THE CLARION CALL

Repentance, Relationship, Revival

LATOSHIA MCKOY

Copyright © 2020 by Latoshia Mckoy All rights reserved

Published by (publisher) No part of this publication may be reproduced, distributed, or transmitted in any form or by any means, including photocopying, recording, or other electronic or mechanical methods, without the prior written permission of the publisher, except in the case of brief quotations embodied in critical reviews and certain other noncommercial uses permitted by copyright law. For permission requests, write to the publisher, addressed "Attention: Permissions Coordinator," at the address below. Limit of Liability/Disclaimer of Warranty: While the publisher and author have used their best efforts in preparing this book, they make no representations of warranties with respect to the accuracy or completeness of the contents of this book and specifically disclaim any implied warranties or merchantability or fitness for a particular purpose. No warranty may be created or extended by sales representatives or written sales materials. The advice and strategies contained herein may not be suitable for your situation. You should consult with a professional where appropriate. Neither the publisher nor author shall be liable for damages arising here from.

Beyond The Book Media, LLC

5174 McGinnis Ferry Rd. Suite 152

Alpharetta, Georgia 30005

www.beyondthebookmedia.com

The publisher is not responsible for websites that are not owned by the publisher.

ISBN –978-1-953788-03-0 (Printed)

Unless otherwise indicated, all scripture quotations are from the Holy Bible, English Standard Version 2016 (ESV), copyright 2001 by Crossway, a publishing ministry of Good News Publishers. ESV Text Edition: 2016. Used by permission. All rights reserved.

CONTENTS

Introduction	v
Ezekiel	ix
Prayer	1
Clarion Call	3
1. Obedience and Repentance	4
Prayer	13
2. Amazing Grace	14
3. Relationship Building a Firm Foundation	17
Prayer	24
4. God Requires a Unified Church	25
Prayer	31
5. Revival	32
Restoration	36
Prayer	37
References	39

INTRODUCTION

I would like to recognize my mother, Patricia Melvin, who was born on July 10, 1956 and transcended into her heavenly home on December 4, 2019.

This is the second book of The Next Level Series. The word that God has given me to share makes me feel like Jonah. I'm going to be obedient because I do not want to have any blood on my hands. In 2007, God touched my life; He called me Priestess. I received my calling and identified my purpose in the body of Christ. It has been a struggle for me to accept who God says that I am. I have ignored, ran from, and neglected my call simply because I could not accept who God says I am. The fact that I neglected my call never changed the mandate on my life; it never changed my purpose. Does that resonate with any of you? How many of us have a problem believing God when he has revealed our purpose? The first book of the Next level series was written in 2013. The struggle was real. In this season, I choose to believe God and walk boldly in the mandate that he has given me.

Even as I am completing this assignment, the whole world has shifted. We are faced with a pandemic of biblical proportions.

The doctors, scientists, and politicians (all the leaders of the world) are on edge, trying to find answers and cures. What are we going to do now? Is this the end of the world as we knew it?

Over the last ten years, I raised my two children as a single mom and served in the capacity of a caregiver for my mother until she passed. I was part of the "Sandwich Generation." The Sandwich Generation takes care of children and parents at the same time. It's a stretch for many families. You work a full-time job and manage to be a caregiver and parent at the same time. My children are now grown up, and I can dedicate more time to myself and ministry.

Right after my mother's death, God repeatedly gave me dreams confirming it was time for me to step out. In one reoccurring dream I've had over the years, I am in the church choir but always forget the words to the song. Recently, I had that dream, but this time, I remembered the words and sang them beautifully. I remember waking up amazed, wondering why this time I knew the words and not all the times before. God has told many of you it is time. It is time to accept your purpose. The mantle has been given to you. It is your turn. It's time.

In another dream, I saw myself in a whirlwind with a baby I was trying to protect. The house blew apart, but angels helped us find safety in the storm. After the storm was over, angels came to help us rebuild and restore. I dreamed of my great grandmother, Estelle. She was watering her flowers on her front porch. I said to her, "Grandma, your flowers are beautiful. How did you get them to be so beautiful?" She said, "Renee, devote." Devote is a very powerful word. When you think about what it means to be totally devoted to things and people, you will find that it is a next-level commitment that forces a person to be steadfast and unmovable.

INTRODUCTION

Losing my mother is one of the most devastating events that has ever taken place in my life. My mom loved God, and she spent her time reading, praying, and praising Him. I contribute that to her beating the odds for years while struggling with several different ailments. The day she died, I peeked into her room to tell her good morning. She was extremely happy. She told me that morning that she had the best time praising the Lord. Later she came down, and we had our breakfast. We loved our coffee and conversation. She didn't mention any pain or discomfort. Later that afternoon, I walked into the kitchen and found my mom deceased. One minute, she was here, and the next minute, she was gone. God called her home without warning. As I write this, I'm still in disbelief.

In January 2020, the world witnessed the sudden death of Kobe Bryant and the other passengers on that flight. Everyone pulled up his last tweet that spoke of his church attendance just before the crash. If you are reading these words, you still have time to be who God has called you to be. Imagine being taken suddenly without warning, without fulfilling your purpose, without being true to who God has predestined you to be.

Before I formed thee in the belly, I knew thee; and before thou camest forth out of the womb, I sanctified thee, and I ordained thee a prophet unto the nations.

— JEREMIAH 1:5 (KJV)

I was traveling out of town to get a break and clear my mind, still grieving the loss of my mother when God began to speak to me regarding racism, division, pollution, and religion. My mental was so full of information about many topics I would not want to discuss because I'm not one to argue. When God gave me the charge to complete this book, I said, "God, these are touchy subjects and offend many ideologies that exist in Christianity and the world. No one wants to talk about these things. People get highly emotional.

"Father, you know I'm not one that argues or enjoys strife. Certainly, God, you don't want little me to tackle these big demons. People live how they live, what can I say or do? Why can't I just be responsible for my family?"

I prayed, and I prayed. At this moment, the mantle was just as heavy as it was with Jeremiah, Jonah, and the other prophets in the Bible who received their assignment from God. I wanted everyone to work out their own soul salvation. After I calmed down and listened to God, I heard Him say, *"You must tell the people what I say to save their life."* Many will not agree with these instructions. God mandates that those of us who have received His instructions be "watchmen." He commands that we sound the trumpet and warn the people in obedience to God.

EZEKIEL

EZEKIEL SOUNDS THE TRUMPET TO WARN THE PEOPLE:

Ezekiel 33:1-11 (KJV)

1 Again the Word of the Lord came unto me, saying,

² Son of man, speak to the children of thy people, and say unto them, When I bring the sword upon a land, if the people of the land take a man of their coasts, and set him for their watchman:

³ If when he seeth the sword come upon the land, he blow the trumpet, and warn the people;

⁴ Then whosoever heareth the sound of the trumpet, and taketh not warning; if the sword come, and take him away, his blood shall be upon his own head.

⁵ He heard the sound of the trumpet, and took not warning; his blood shall be upon him. But he that taketh warning shall deliver his soul.

⁶ But if the watchman see the sword come, and blow not the trumpet, and the people be not warned; if the sword come, and take any person from among them, he is taken away in his iniquity; but his blood will I require at the watchman's hand.

⁷ So thou, O son of man, I have set thee a watchman unto the house of Israel; therefore, thou shalt hear the Word at my mouth, and warn them from me.

⁸ When I say unto the wicked, O wicked man, thou shalt surely die; if thou dost not speak to warn the wicked from his way, that wicked man shall die in his iniquity; but his blood will I require at thine hand.

⁹ Nevertheless, if thou warn the wicked of his way to turn from it; if he does not turn from his way, he shall die in his iniquity; but thou hast delivered thy soul.

¹⁰ Therefore, O thou son of man, speak unto the house of Israel; Thus, ye speak, saying, if our transgressions and our sins be upon us, and we pine away in them, how should we then live?

¹¹ Say unto them, As I live, saith the Lord God, I have no pleasure in the death of the wicked; but that the wicked turn from his way and live: turn ye, turn ye from your evil ways; for why will ye die, O house of Israel?"

I am sounding my trumpet; I must warn the people. If I don't warn you in obedience to God, I am responsible for your sin. God, did I get that right? I will be responsible for the sin of man! So, I decided to write and promote this message. In America and around the world, God says people are committing sins openly and in their hearts against their brother. All trees rooted in sin will be cut off from Him. The sin of racism, bigotry, division, strife, jealousy, murder, greed, perversion, and unforgiveness will prevent you from experiencing eternal life.

God gave me the vision of an old oak tree. If you know anything about oak trees, you know they have many branches and can live for hundreds of years. God said these oak trees have sinful roots. They are rooted in racism, bigotry, jealousy, slander, rape, murder, greed, and perversion. God says He is going to cut these trees off. These trees and their branches represent families and establishments that will be cut off because they have been rooted in sin and have not changed. Bitter fruit grows from these trees.

Hear the trumpet sound! It is time to repent, develop a relationship with God, and restore yourselves in preparation for the coming of our Savior, the Lord Jesus Christ.

PRAYER

Dear Heavenly Father,

I asked that you bless the words on these pages. I pray that you prepare the hearts and minds of the readers to receive in love what you have to say in these pages. Lord, we pray that love wins. We pray that unity wins within the body of Christ all around the world. Lord, we desire to become all that you would require. Jesus, we want to dwell with you for eternity. We welcome your Holy Spirit to minister to our hearts through these pages. We caste down pride, disobedience, and rebellion.

In Jesus' Holy name, we pray.

Amen.

CLARION CALL

"For the foundation of the earth is the Lord's. On them, he has set the world."

This is a time of renewal and replenishing.

This is a time to establish divine order and justice.

This is a time to uncover truth and divine wisdom

Will we be ready when the trumpets sound?

Will we have found a relationship with the Most High?

Will we know the mystery of our existence?

Help us, God, to understand your divine plan

Help us live a life that Glorifies you

Help us live out our purpose

CHAPTER 1
OBEDIENCE AND REPENTANCE

Life should prepare you for the Kingdom. God's teachers should be sharing the Good News of Jesus Christ -- why He lived, why He died, and how He rose again. We should be taught how to prepare our souls for our heavenly home and live a life that reflects Christ on earth. The church buildings are empty. Some will argue that the COVID-19 pandemic was not sent by God. I can't say that it was. However, the world is the Lord's and the fullness thereof. God is in control. The pandemic would not exist if God did not allow it to exist. As Christians, that is what we believe, if we believe the Bible in its entirety. God warned us in the Bible about things that are now coming to pass.

I am a mother of two children. I love them deeply and will lay down my life for them. With all the love I have for my children, it can't compare to the perfect love that God has for his children. Through our experience as a parent and a child, we know the importance of obedience. How many times have we disobeyed our parents and suffered the consequences of our actions? Rules made from love are normally made for our protection, and when we break them, it leads to harm to ourselves or others.

God reminded me of a time when I was around 15 years old and wanted to fit in with the cool kids. My grandmother had raised me in the church. She had laid a firm foundation for me. Coming into my teenage years, I rejected that. I wanted to have fun and hang with the in-crowd. I stopped participating in church, and my church attendance fell off.

One day I decided to go to my friend's house because if I hung out with her, she could expose me to the cool people. The hang out spot was called The Wild Side, and that is exactly what it was. You could gamble and buy and sell drugs and alcohol. This is where the cool people hung out.

Someone passing by the house saw me and went to tell my grandmother. In less than ten minutes of me being there, she was pulling up. She walked into that house and made me leave. I was upset and didn't want to leave. I was so naïve. I didn't realize the danger I was in. I just wanted to fit in. I wanted to be around drug dealers because they had flashy cars, jewelry, and money. At that moment, I didn't have a clue.

Now I look back and give God glory that she loved me so much. My grandmother wasn't afraid to walk into the drug house to save me from things I knew nothing of. So many souls were lost to drugs, crime, death, and prison. The enemy could have destroyed me because I willingly walked into his camp.

God is grieving just like my grandmother did when she found out her only grandchild had stumbled blindly into the enemy's camp. The enemy awaits to steal, kill, and destroy. When we leave God's secret place, we remove ourselves from His shadow. The devil can destroy us. The church is moving away from God's secret place and into the world.

When we compromise God's word for personal gain or to fit into the worlds' way of doing things, that is exactly what we are doing. We are not to change or package the church in worldly wrapping paper to win souls. The soul is to be transformed and renewed to become like Christ. If souls are not being prepared for the Kingdom of God, everything is void.

We may hear inspiring messages about wealth, but if we measure these messages against God's word, would they come up short? Believers measure the message against God's word. The Bible is your measuring stick. This would require that you read the Bible yourself to see what God says in full about the matter.

Sunday after Sunday, we have heard how God is going to bless the cheerful giver. Scripture will back that up; however, living in sin and being disobedient will not allow you to reap the full blessings of God without consequence. Wealth in this world is nice but temporary. So why have we endured the feel-good hype many megachurches have been built by for decades?

God gave his children the Ten Commandments. When I was growing up, these commandments were found posted up in homes, churches, and government buildings. I challenge us to locate them posted anywhere today.

In the Book of Exodus, God delivered his children from bondage. They had witnessed miracles, His wrath, and His love for them. God delivered them from the hands of their enemies.

During this time, God gave them ten rules that would glorify him and prevent us from hurting ourselves and others. We are still under this covenant and responsible for following these commandments.

Now, therefore, if ye obey my voice indeed, and keep my covenant, then ye shall be a peculiar treasure unto me above all people: for all the earth is mine.

— *EXODUS 19:5 (KJV)*

The 10 Commandments
Exodus 20:3-17 *(KJV)*

- *Thou shalt have no other Gods before me*
- *Thou shalt not make unto thee any graven image or any likeness of anything that is in heaven above, or that is in the earth beneath, or that is in water under the earth. Thou shalt not bow down thyself to them. Nor serve them: for I the Lord they God am a jealous God, visiting the iniquity of the fathers upon the children unto the third and fourth generation of them that hate and showing mercy unto thousands of them that love me and keep my commandments.*
- *Thou shalt not take the name of the Lord thy God in vain; for the Lord will not hold him guiltless that taketh his name in vain.*
- *Remember the Sabbath day and keep it Holy, Six days shalt thy labor and do all thy work: but the seventh day is the Sabbath of the Lord thy God: in it, thou shalt not do any work, thou, nor thy maidservant, nor thy cattle, nor thy stranger that is within thy gates: for in six days the Lord made heaven and earth, the sea, and all that in them is and rested the seventh day: wherefore the Lord blessed and Sabbath day, and hallowed it.*
- *Honor thy Father and thy mother: that thy days may be long upon the land which the Lord thy God giveth thee.*
- *Thou shalt not kill*
- *Thou shalt not commit adultery*
- *Thou shalt not steal*
- *Thou shalt not bear false witness against thy neighbor.*

- *Thou shalt not covet thy neighbor's wife, or his ox, or his ass, or anything that is thy neighbors.*

Obedience is better than sacrifice

> *And Samuel said, Hath the LORD as great delight in burnt offerings and sacrifices, as in obeying the voice of the LORD? Behold, to obey is better than sacrifice, and to hearken than the fat of rams.*
>
> *— 1 SAMUEL 15:22(KJV)*

You can't pay your way into the Kingdom. Only obedience will get you in. God requires our obedience to and His ways. It's obedience over everything. When we operate in obedience, we line up with God's will for our lives. The power and blessings that manifest when operating in obedience can't be denied. The earth is the Lord's and the fulness thereof; your money doesn't move Him. It's a vain sacrifice if you live in disobedience.

Repentance

True obedience will lead us to repent for our sins and make a sincere effort to sin no more. We are all guilty of sin and rely upon God's grace and mercy. We show our love towards God by striving to be obedient. Jesus came to fulfill the law, and He died for our sins to be forgiven, but He didn't die to give us an open invitation to abuse his grace. The nature of God is distorted when we feel that we can live a life of sin because Jesus died for us. While performing street evangelism, I have been faced with the phrase "Jesus came for the sinner. He's coming back for me the sinner, not church folks." I've heard it several times, and each time, I'm stunned. I never hesitate to deliver the news that we will not enter the Kingdom of Heaven if we do not sincerely repent. I stress sincerely because God knows our hearts.

The trumpet has sounded! REPENT!

Sanctification

> *Sanctify them through thy truth: thy word is truth.*
>
> — JOHN 17:17 *(KJV)*

In John Chapter 17, Jesus prays to God during the final hours before He was crucified. This prayer explains who Jesus is, who we are, and who God is. I often call it "The Lord's Prayer." I would encourage every believer to meditate on John 17 because it also establishes "Purpose."

John 17:1–26 (KJV)

¹ These words spake Jesus, and lifted up his eyes to heaven, and said, Father, the hour is come; glorify thy Son, that thy Son also may glorify thee:

² As thou hast given him power over all flesh, that he should give eternal life to as many as thou hast given him.

³ And this is life eternal, that they might know thee the only true God, and Jesus Christ, whom thou hast sent.

⁴ I have glorified thee on the earth: I have finished the work which thou gavest me to do.

⁵ And now, O Father, glorify thou me with thine own self with the glory which I had with thee before the world was.

⁶ I have manifested thy name unto the men which thou gavest me out of the world: thine they were, and thou gavest them me; and they have kept thy Word.

⁷ Now they have known that all things whatsoever thou hast given me are of thee.

⁸ For I have given unto them the words which thou gavest me; and they have received them, and have known surely that I came out from thee, and they have believed that thou didst send me.

⁹ I pray for them: I pray not for the world, but for them which thou hast given me; for they are thine.

¹⁰ And all mine are thine, and thine are mine; and I am glorified in them.

¹¹ And now I am no more in the world, but these are in the world, and I come to thee. Holy Father, keep through thine own name those whom thou hast given me, that they may be one, as we are.

¹² While I was with them in the world, I kept them in thy name: those that thou gavest me I have kept, and none of them is lost, but the son of perdition; that the scripture might be fulfilled.

¹³ And now come I to thee; and these things I speak in the world, that they might have my joy fulfilled in themselves.

¹⁴ I have given them thy word; and the world hath hated them, because they are not of the world, even as I am not of the world.

¹⁵ I pray not that thou shouldest take them out of the world, but that thou shouldest keep them from the evil.

¹⁶ They are not of the world, even as I am not of the world.

¹⁷ Sanctify them through thy truth: thy word is truth.

¹⁸ As thou hast sent me into the world, even so have I also sent them into the world.

¹⁹ And for their sakes I sanctify myself, that they also might be sanctified through the truth.

²⁰ Neither pray I for these alone, but for them also which shall believe on me through their word;

²¹ That they all may be one; as thou, Father, art in me, and I in thee, that they also may be one in us: that the world may believe that thou hast sent me.

²² And the glory which thou gavest me I have given them; that they may be one, even as we are one:

²³ I in them, and thou in me, that they may be made perfect in one; and that the world may know that thou hast sent me, and hast loved them, as thou hast loved me.

²⁴ Father, I will that they also, whom thou hast given me, be with me where I am; that they may behold my glory, which thou hast given me: for thou loved me before the foundation of the world.

²⁵ O righteous Father, the world hath not known thee: but I have known thee, and these have known that thou hast sent me.

²⁶ And I have declared unto them thy name and will declare it: that the love wherewith thou hast loved me may be in them, and I in them.

As believers, we must know and live out the Word of God. The Bible is referred to as a GPS that will give us directions to eternal life. We must sanctify ourselves with God's word because:

1. It is a Blueprint for the body of Christ
2. It provides Godly wisdom and instruction
3. It provides assurance, peace, and joy

Holy Spirit

But the Comforter, which is the Holy Ghost, whom the Father will send in my name, he shall teach you all things, and bring all things to your remembrance, whatsoever I have said unto you.

— JOHN 14:26 (KJV)

Cast me not away from thy presence; and take not thy Holy Spirit from me.

— PSALM 51:11 (KJV)

GOD The Father, GOD the Son, and GOD The Holy Spirit are one. The Holy Spirit is God within us. The Holy Spirit speaks to the believer and the non-believer; the Holy Spirit is GOD. Both believers and non-believers reject the Holy Spirit. Rejecting the Holy Spirit is to reject GOD. Rejecting the Holy Spirit is an act or acts of disobedience to God. The Holy Spirit is the source of conviction.

PRAYER

Dear Heavenly Father

We repent of our sins. We desire to walk in alignment with you. Lord, give me the strength and wisdom to overcome temptation, resist our flesh, and work in obedience to your will, not our will. Heavenly Father, may your will be done. Help us, Heavenly Father, to fix our mind on heavenly things, good thoughts. Help us, Heavenly Father, in our areas of weakness, make us strong. Lead us and guide us, Lord, that we stay on your narrow path. Have mercy on us, Father.

Help us, Lord, to reflect your magnificent glory on this earth. Restore us, God, unto you that we may walk in boldness, faith, and power.

In Jesus' name, we pray.

Amen

CHAPTER 2
AMAZING GRACE

Redemption

Shortly after the death of Kobe Bryant, I decided to take a road trip. I was stressed, grieving, and dealing with the onset of a health condition. I was listening to the radio, and they mentioned that Usher sang "Amazing Grace" during one of the basketball games as a tribute to Kobe. That hymn is timeless. It is The story of a sinner who was forgiven. That is every believer's story because it resonates with the truth. We all have sinned and fallen short of the Glory of God.

I began to think about the sin of unforgiveness. Why is it so hard to forgive when we know that no one is perfect? To go deeper, I thought about the origin of the song. The writer was a minister who once participated in the Transatlantic Slave Trade.

The writer of Amazing Grace, John Newton, received his foundation from his Christian mother. His mother died from tuberculosis when he was only seven years old. By age 11, he had a job on a merchant ship. John Newton was described as an unruly individual who lacked discipline. In 1747 while out at sea, a terrible storm arose. He almost lost his life in that storm, but he pledged his life to Christ and gained it. John Newton later became instrumental in the movement to abolish slavery. As long as we're breathing, we can be redeemed. The thief on the cross beside Jesus was redeemed. It does not matter the sin or past mistakes. Every soul can be redeemed. In the Bible, Paul condemned the church to death before his encounter with Jesus on the Road to Damascus. Do not allow the bad judgment and mistakes of your past prevent you from repenting and being redeemed.

Amazing Grace By: John Newton

Amazing Grace! How sweet the sound
That saved a wretch like me!
I once was lost, but now am found
Was blind, but now I see.
'Twas Grace that taught my heart to fear,
And grace my fears relieved.
How precious did that grace appear
The hour I first believed.
Through many dangers, toils, and snares
I have already come.
'Tis Grace hath brought me safe thus far
And grace will lead me home.
The Lord has promised good to me.
His Word my hope secures.
He will my shield and portion be
As long as life endures.
When we've been there ten thousand years
Bright shining as the sun,
We've no less days to sing God's praise
Than when we'd first begun.

To open their eyes, and to turn them from darkness to light, and from the power of Satan unto God, that they may receive forgiveness of sins, and inheritance among them which are sanctified by faith that is in me.

— *ACTS 26:18 (KJV)*

I have blotted out, as a thick cloud, thy transgressions, and, as a cloud, thy sins: return unto me; for I have redeemed thee.

— *ISAIAH 44:22 (KJV)*

The trumpet has sounded: May the Redeemed of the Lord say so!

CHAPTER 3

RELATIONSHIP BUILDING A FIRM FOUNDATION

Many of us were exposed to Christianity early in life. We were raised in a Christian household and attended church services, bible study, revival, conferences, and all the other church meetings in between on a regular basis. We can recall all the bible stories. David and Goliath. Daniel in the Lion's Den. My favorite was the story of Meshach, Shadrach, and Abednego. Every minister would add their twist and give us an interpretation. It was very uplifting, and we would leave church feeling good!

What about those of us who did not attend church? Many practice other religions, including voodoo and witchcraft. People who are atheists do not believe in a higher power, only logic and science. Some Africans born in America feel robbed and disconnected from their spirituality and distrust the things we have been taught to believe in. Sometimes the only point of reference is the people that profess the faith.

If we lack wisdom, ask God!

When we gain wisdom, how do we apply the information to our everyday walk?

Is it possible for us to be in church, yet the church not be in us?

The foundation of our faith will shape and strengthen us as we make this Christian journey. A builder must locate the land first. Then he performs due diligence to make sure the location is solid, preferably in a no flood zone. The builder knows to be very careful constructing the foundation. If it is not done properly, anything that he builds on will be subject to cracking and shifting. Our souls are no different. If we don't do our due diligence, we will crack and shift. Without a sturdy foundation, the entire building is no good.

A firm foundation will remain, even if everything else crumbles. Throughout the Bible, we see that God would allow the temple to be destroyed and reconstructed. In this present day, we see things have gone off course, and shame has been bestowed on the body of Christ. The body of Christ is constantly under attack for operating immorally. It is very necessary to start over, starting with reaffirming a firm foundation.

> *And I say also unto thee, that thou art Peter, and upon this rock I will build my church; and the gates of hell shall not prevail against it.*
>
> — *MATTHEW 16:18 (KJV)*

Formal Introduction

Children of God Meet God the Father, Creator of Heaven and Earth, Alpha and Omega, The Great "I AM"

A firm foundation requires that we not only know who God is, but we also have a personal relationship with our Father. I didn't grow up in a home with my father. I knew who he was, and he knew I existed. Unfortunately, we never developed a close relationship. Personal relationships consist of checking in on each other daily and frequent communication. The father has the role of loving, protecting, and providing for their children. The children's role is to be loving, obedient, serve, and show gratitude to their father. Every new day, hour, minute, and second holds an opportunity to start over and rebuild a relationship, but misunderstandings, lack of communication, fear, pride, and unforgiveness often prevent that from occurring.

God would like to have a relationship with his children. Unlike our natural fathers, he is omnipresent and knows more about us than we know about ourselves. How much do we know about God? Do we read our Bible? Do we pray? Do we listen? Do we obey? In Genesis, we see how God created the heavens, earth, and mankind. Our trouble began in the Garden of Eden. Sin and suffering were not part of God's original design.

I've had experience witnessing about God in a homeless shelter, on the street, and in parks. The people were addicted, mentally ill, disabled, and impoverished. They're still God's children, even though they are in an unfavorable condition. They had real questions. Who is God? Why do we need Jesus? They made statements regarding church hurt and Christians who did not look like their father. They had questions that stemmed from a lack of a personal relationship with God. Much like my relationship with my natural father, they neglected to get to know God for themselves. If we don't know God, it's impossible for us to have faith. Faith in God activates power and blessings. Get to know God by reading the Bible, praying, fasting, and communicating constantly. The more attention we give God, the more we will see his presence manifest in our lives.

Clean Slate

I am terrible with laptops and cell phones. My very first laptop crashed after eight months. I had no idea what to do. I downloaded so many viruses trying to listen to free music and watch free movies. What a waste. It ran slower and slower until it finally crashed.

Many of us are like my computer. We have downloaded so much bad doctrine and incorrect information that we're on the brink of crashing. Are we at the point where we no longer know what to believe? Should I tithe or not? What is prosperity? Why am I not rich? What is a seed? Is the Bible real? Is Jesus real? Was Jesus the son of God or a Prophet? Is Israel the chosen people of God? Is the Old Testament relevant?

Many of us have been dedicated to the church, and we love our pastor. But hold up. Wait… I just found out the pastor is not perfect. The pastor just stole all the money from the church. Others of us have tried to serve but didn't fit into the church clique. They rejected us, and we no longer attend. Many of us are running slow or have already crashed.

Just like that computer, we need to start over. Go back to the original settings. Delete every download until we are back to the beginning with only what the manufacturer (God) provided.

God is the Creator of all things. When we develop a personal relationship with God, we can avoid many mishaps along our Christian journey. We don't have to rely on anyone else to feed us His Word because we read the Bible for ourselves with the Holy Spirit as our teacher and guide. This is not to say you should not attend church. I just believe we should seek God every day, not only on Sunday mornings. We don't need intersession because we pray to God for ourselves and others. The body of Christ is the intercessor for the world. This relationship will prevent us from following the wrong doctrine. We can recognize when someone is using witchcraft or promoting false doctrine because we are reading and studying God's Word on our own time.

Jesus the Chief Cornerstone

Let's build the relationship with Jesus Christ, the one who died for our sins, is the source of our salvation and the foundation of our faith.

I went through a divorce as a Christian, and it shook my foundation. I felt like a complete fraud and a failure. Mostly, I felt condemned that I had disappointed God. As time went by, I felt God's love, presence, guidance, and provision like never before. Is it not amazing that I messed up, but God didn't leave my side? During this dark period, I felt the presence of God like never before. At that time, the enemy wanted me to believe that God had turned his back on me because of my sin.

I separated from my husband with what I could fit in my small Chevy Malibu and my two children. I had found a job before we left, and a friend agreed to allow us to stay with them until I found a place to live. I soon found a small single-family house but, at the same time, found that my start date for my new job would be pushed back a month. I had paid my deposit but only had enough money for one month's rent. I had to swallow my pride and borrow that from a family member.

Just when I thought things were moving in the right direction, I received a call my brother had been murdered in his home. The killers were unknown and on the loose. Early the next morning, I received a knock on the door; it was the repo man. I got my belongings out of the car because we hadn't had a chance to unload it yet. Then I watched the repo man drive off. *How will I attend my brother's funeral that was a two-hour drive away?*

I was right in the middle of losing my mind when God used an earthly angel that allowed me to borrow an extra car and even gave me a black dress to wear to the funeral. Another friend purchased a cell phone, and the first month of service. It's good to have a friend when we need a friend. No one can make it in this world alone. With every punch, God had a counter punch to meet every need. The punches kept coming, and God kept fighting my battles until this very day.

The enemy was working overtime. It was only recently that people began to share all the lies and gossip with me. It was unbelievable. However, because of the personal relationships I built over the years, people did not believe what they heard. When we know someone personally, people can't make us believe something that is out of character for that individual.

The people we befriend become our character witnesses. In the event we are ever accused of anything unlawful, the court will subpoena our character witnesses. Those witnesses can tell others about all our good deeds and our kind heart. Right now, the body of Christ is being served a court summons to be character witnesses for Christ. I shared a little of my testimony to glorify God. We must do this so that non-believers will know who God is. Be pro-Christ and spread to Good News. Don't sit on the testimony that God has given us.

> *For God so loved the world, that he gave his only begotten Son, that whosoever believeth in him should not perish, but have everlasting life.*
>
> — *JOHN 3:16 (KJV)*

The keyword that stands out to me in this scripture is whosoever. I made up my mind to be whosoever. It doesn't matter what people call us or what we've done in our past. When we make up our minds to believe that Jesus Christ is the son of God, and he died for us to be saved, we become *whosoever*.

Jesus Bore All Our Iniquities Out of Love and Amazing Grace.

Isaiah 42:1-4 (KJV)

Behold my servant, whom I uphold; mine elect, in whom my soul delighteth; I have put my Spirit upon him: he shall bring forth judgment to the Gentiles.

² He shall not cry, nor lift up, nor cause his voice to be heard in the street.

³ A bruised reed shall he not break, and the smoking flax shall he not quench: he shall bring forth judgment unto truth.

⁴ He shall not fail nor be discouraged, till he has set judgment in the earth: and the isles shall wait for his law.

Isaiah is a prophet that received these words directly from God. God told Isaiah Our Savior was coming.

PRAYER

Dear Heavenly Father,

We pray for a stronger relationship with you. We pray and ask your forgiveness for all the times we did not seek your face. Forgive us, Heavenly Father, for our neglect. We pray that we continue to be mindful of you. Help us to resist the devil and the distractions that take us away from you. Heavenly Father, give us the courage to tell others about you that they may also seek to have a relationship with you.

In Jesus' name, I pray.

Amen.

CHAPTER 4
GOD REQUIRES A UNIFIED CHURCH

We are one Spirit and called to operate on one accord.

1 Corinthians 12:12-27 (KJV)

12 For as the body is one, and hath many members, and all the members of that one body, being many, are one body: so also is Christ.

13 For by one Spirit are we all baptized into one body, whether we be Jews or Gentiles, whether we be bond or free; and have been all made to drink into one Spirit.

14 For the body is not one member, but many.

15 If the foot shall say, Because I am not the hand, I am not of the body; is it therefore not of the body?

16 And if the ear shall say, Because I am not the eye, I am not of the body; is it therefore not of the body?

17 If the whole body were an eye, where were the hearing? If the whole were hearing, where were the smelling?

18 But now hath God set the members every one of them in the body, as it hath pleased him.

¹⁹ And if they were all one member, where were the body?

²⁰ But now are they many members, yet but one body.

²¹ And the eye cannot say unto the hand, I have no need of thee: nor again the head to the feet, I have no need of you.

²² Nay, much more those members of the body, which seem to be more feeble, are necessary:

²³ And those members of the body, which we think to be less honorable, upon these we bestow more abundant honor; and our uncomely parts have more abundant comeliness.

²⁴ For our comely parts have no need: but God hath tempered the body together, having given more abundant honor to that part which lacked.

²⁵ That there should be no schism in the body; but that the members should have the same care one for another. ²⁶ And whether one member suffer, all the members suffer with it; or one member be honored, all the members rejoice with it. ²⁷ Now ye are the body of Christ, and members in particular.

Imagine going to a football game as a spectator. You are watching your favorite team play. You cheer when they make a touchdown. You criticize them when they throw an interception or miss a field goal. Currently, in the body of Christ, we have spectators and those who are in the game. The players learn the rules of the game, go to practice, maintain a physical condition, adhere to a certain diet and routine to play the game. The spectator doesn't do anything but show up, watch, cheer, criticize, and watch the highlights of ESPN. God is calling a time out. It's time for spectators to get in the game. It's easy to criticize others when they make a mistake or use poor judgment. It's time that we all get in the game and support the team. We all have a position to perfect and play. What is your part in the body of Christ? If you see an area of weakness, address it, and improve. Build with the team.

Unity within the body of Christ is what our God requires. If one member suffers, all the members suffer. If one member is honored, we all should rejoice.

After meditating on the song Amazing Grace and the story behind its composer, I asked God why we have so much division within the church. We have different denominations. We still have predominately black and white churches. Even moral matters are causing a divide. *God, why do we see this within the body of Christ?*

God began to minister to me by the Holy Spirit. He took me to the beginning of Genesis because He is the Creator of everything. He created everyone, and because no one is the same, He created people with different features, strengths, gifts, and spiritual abilities. He did the same with every beast in the field, ocean, and sky.

Race should have never become an issue. The Holy Spirit explained people have made an issue about and created division over things that never mattered. What matters to God is that we love each other and not sin against one another. This is the standard God has for his church. It is the sinful nature of man that determines the character, not a physical appearance.

We are all one body when we surrender our lives to Christ. Today, no one wants to tackle the real conversations. Everything is masked in political correctness. God did not give us the Spirit of fear, and the challenge of today is to be transparent about what God requires. It is too late in the evening to consider or fear the backlash from the world. God's Kingdom and this world can't operate the same. The prince of this world is Satan. Why are we trying so hard to look like Satan?

There is no power in a lukewarm, watered-down church. The shepherd will be responsible for leading all those people to a ditch because he didn't teach obedience, repentance, love, unity, and Kingdom. I gave my life to Christ after the world used me and abused me. Every sin had a negative consequence. "I was sinking deep in sin." When I gave my life to God, that changed. I had trials, but I overcame them. I have peace and reassurance. A change came over me.

"Divide and Conquer" is an old tactic. God requires his church to be in alignment with him and be unified. There is only one message, and it hasn't changed. God requires that we stick to His Word, his manual the GPS to heaven. We need to stand firm and not be blown to and from.

Today we face a pandemic. Many debates surround this virus. Is COVID-19 a democrat or republican? Is COVID-19 man-made? Is COVID-19 a hoax? Should we have church in the building or virtual church? Should we open the economy or be safe and wait? There is a different viewpoint for each question. Why can't we agree? The inability to agree causes strife and division. That is what the enemy and prince of this world enjoys. The longer we spend in disagreement, the more he can steal, kill, and destroy.

Looking Back

In 1773, the First African Baptist Church was organized on the Brampton Plantation in Savannah, Georgia. Presiding Pastor George Leile, a slave, was the first licensed by the Baptist to preach in Georgia. He traveled to plantations preaching to slaves converting and baptizing them in the coastal Georgia and South Carolina area. He was freed during the revolutionary war. When Britain lost the war, he was evacuated to Jamaica and became the first missionary in Jamaica.

Andrew Bryan, a member of the church, took over as pastor with 67 members in 1788. They continued to hold the services at the Brampton barn on the plantation. The 3rd pastor was

Andrew Cox Marshall, the nephew of Andrew Bryan. In 1832, Pastor Marshall went to the congregation with a vision he had from God to build a church made of bricks. Pastor Marshall knew of a white church that was selling a parcel of land for $1500.00. He shared his vision with a congregation of enslaved Africans. The enslaved Africans were saving money to purchase their freedom and the freedom of family members.

Dilemma: Do we keep our money or buy the land for a church? For many of us, that would be a no brainer. We would keep our money and have services in the barn. Just to be honest, we can imagine freedom was something they dreamed of day and night. The average cost of a slave at that time was $800.00. The cost depended on the age, size, and gender of the slave. The cost of freedom could have been a little more; it was at the slave owners' discretion.

The congregation decided to (drum roll) purchase the land for the church. They came up with $1000.00 and agreed to pay the other $500.00 within six months, in which they did. They made a wooden building and worshiped in it until 1855.

In 1855, they tore down the wood building and began building a brick structure. The slaveholders agreed to allow them to build the church after they had completed their work on the plantation. They worked on the building at night. The men and the women worked together. Men could not be caught roaming the city at night. The women were given the job of collecting the bricks. The bricks were made down by the river, so the women toted the bricks in their aprons up an incline to the church site. The women also had to keep a barn fire lit so the men could see at night.

In 1859, the largest slave auction in US history took place in Savannah, "The Weeping Time." I visited Savannah to do a tour of the church. During that time, a ceremony was being held to commemorate what transpired 160 years ago. On March 2-3, 1859, 900 slaves were auctioned. Rain fell until the last slave was sold (The Weeping Time).

This church became part of the Underground Railroad from 1859 until January 12, 1865, when the Emancipation Proclamation was acknowledged in Savannah. Slaves were hidden underneath the floors of the church. Deacon Hayes was the conductor, and over 3000 slaves used that church as a gateway to freedom.

This is how God will need us to operate in this season. The church was neither black nor white; everyone played a role. Abolitionists, bond and freed slaves, freed over 3000 slaves in unity and obedience.

PRAYER

Dear Heavenly Father

I pray for unity within your church. God, we pray that minor things do not separate us. We pray that every church uses the Word of God as the standard for Kingdom living and preparation. Jesus, we pray that our hearts desire to be more like you, not more like the world. God, your church is and should always be a place where sinners can come and be set free. Be made whole. Be washed with the blood of Christ and start anew. Lord, we pray that we remain close to you and manifest your redeeming power everywhere we go. In our homes, on our jobs, in our communities, in the house of God. We pray your Holy Spirit goes with us everywhere we go. We are praying for souls to be saved by the multitudes in this season. God, we pray that your Spirit will unite all hearts and minds in the body of Christ so that we can see your power manifest in these turbulent days.

In Jesus' name,

Amen

CHAPTER 5
REVIVAL

Wilt thou not revive us again: that thy people may rejoice in thee? -- Psalm 85:6 (KJV)

After the body has repented and turned from darkness, God will heal the land.

> *If my people, which are called by my name, shall humble themselves, and pray, and seek my face, and turn from their wicked ways; then will I hear from heaven, and will forgive their sin, and will heal their land.*
>
> — *2 CHRONICLES 7:14*

God is coming back for his bride, a church without spot or blemish. The only way to make it into the Kingdom is to live for the Kingdom.

> That he might present it to himself a glorious church, not having spot, or wrinkle, or any such thing; but that it should be holy and without blemish.
>
> — *EPHESIANS 5:27 (KJV)*

We have a Kingdom mandate

Seek God First

> *Seek ye first the Kingdom of God, and his righteousness; and all these things shall be added unto you.*
>
> — *MATTHEW 6:33 (KJV)*

In this present day, it appears the world influences the Kingdom than the Kingdom influences the world. How do we win souls to Christ, offering them a lifestyle they already have in the world? In these days, we must unite and remain steadfast on the Word of God without wavering and without compromise. God will show himself mighty, and the church will be powerful.

In 1720, The Great Awakening, inspired by Minister John Edwards and Minister George Whitefield, called for a revival in the church. The Great Awakening Movement of the 1700s reminded the colonies of the importance of having Christ in their lives. In addition, it influenced many governmental institutions.

Important points at that time where:

- All people are born into sin.
- If you don't accept Jesus as your Savior, you will not go to heaven.
- To be saved, you must confess your sins to God and repent.
- Everyone can have a personal relationship with God. The Great Awakening, led by the church, influenced government and institutions.

An "Amazing Grace" Revival of an even greater magnitude is required today. The devil's methods have not changed. He still aims to divide people over matters without seeking God about them. This is not pleasing to God. The Word of God stands firm as the authority in the body of Christ. The secular or worldly way has attempted to penetrate the church since the beginning. The devil has found the church is sleeping and drunk off sin and misguided ideology. In this hour, God requires that we renew our dedication to the Kingdom and renounce the influence of this world. The Kingdom of God is to influence the world, not vice versa.

There is no power or deliverance when the church operates like the world.

There are many benefits to a unified body of Christ and even more benefits to a unified body of Christ that is in alignment with God.

Do we want war, plagues, famine, and locusts? Or our manna from heaven, resurrection of the dead, blind to see, lame to walk, deaf to hear, demons cast out?

While much of the current gospel preached has been centered around prosperity and material wealth, there are so many things that money cannot buy. The most valuable things in life cannot be bought. Seek ye first the Kingdom. God requires our full attention, a revival. We must stop bickering among ourselves long enough to hear from heaven.

The trumpet is blowing. God's children must fall into formation under his grace and His Word. God is calling for a unified church that operates on one accord. He is not interested in black or white, democrat or republican; He created everyone. He is not concerned about denominations. He requires that we unite, stand firm, and be on one accord.

The earth is the Lord's and the fullness thereof

If you hear the trumpet sound, shout halleluiah!!!! Glory to God. It's going to be greater!!! Are you ready to see souls delivered and people healed from diseases? I am.

RESTORATION

Consider our ways.
The current state of the body of Christ
A remnant will obey the voice of God and restore the church
God will be with them.
God will stir up their Spirit.
They will do the work and restore the body of Christ.
The glory of the latter house,
Will be greater than that of the former house.
In this place, God will give us peace.

PRAYER

Heavenly Father,

We repent of our sins. We desire to walk in alignment with you. God help us to resist temptation and our flesh and walk in obedience to your will. Heavenly Father, may your will be done. Help us, Lord, to reflect your magnificent glory on this earth. Restore us, God, so that we may walk in boldness, faith, and power.

In Jesus' name, we pray.

Amen

REFERENCES

Foundation By Latoshia Renee, Outskirts Press Parker CO2013

King James Version Bible Gateway

Christianhistorytoday.com retrieved 4/26/2020

https://www.history.com/topics/british-history/great-awakening retrieved 4/26/20

https://www.soulofamerica.com/us-cities/savannah/first-black-baptist-church/ retrieved 4/26/20

www.ingramcontent.com/pod-product-compliance
Lightning Source LLC
Chambersburg PA
CBHW051712090426
42736CB00013B/2661